Your first 100 words in

KOREAN

Beginner's Quick & Easy Guide to Demystifying Korean Script

Series concept
Jane Wightwick

Illustrations
Mahmoud Gaafar

Korean edition
Heejin Lee

PASSPORT BOOKS
NTC/Contemporary Publishing Group

Other titles in this series:

Your First 100 Words in Arabic
Your First 100 Words in Chinese
Your First 100 Words in Greek
Your First 100 Words in Hebrew
Your First 100 Words in Japanese
Your First 100 Words in Russian

Cover design by Nick Panos

Published by Passport Books
A division of NTC/Contemporary Publishing Group, Inc.
4255 West Touhy Avenue, Lincolnwood (Chicago), Illinois 60712-1975 U.S.A.
Copyright © 2001 by Gaafar & Wightwick
Printed in the United States of America
International Standard Book Number: 0-658-01140-5
2 3 4 5 6 7 8 9 VLP/VLP 0 5 4 3 2 1

CONTENTS

Introduction   4

Scriptbreaker (how the script works)   5

Topics

1 AROUND THE HOME   9
2 CLOTHES   14
3 AROUND TOWN   19
4 COUNTRYSIDE   24
5 OPPOSITES   29
6 ANIMALS   34
7 PARTS OF THE BODY   39
8 USEFUL EXPRESSIONS   44

Round-up (review section)   49

Answers   59

Flashcards (8 sheets of tear-out topic flashcards)

INTRODUCTION

In this activity book you'll find 100 key words for you to learn to read in Korean. All of the activities are designed specifically for reading non-Latin script languages. Many of the activities are inspired by the kind of games used to teach children to read their own language: flashcards, matching games, memory games, joining exercises, etc. This is not only a more effective method of learning to read a new script, but also much more fun.

We've included a **Scriptbreaker** to get you started. This is a friendly introduction to the Korean script that will give you tips on how to remember the letters.

Then you can move on to the 8 **Topics**. Each topic presents essential words in large type. There is also a pronunciation guide so you know how to say the words. These words are also featured in the tear-out **Flashcard** section at the back of the book. When you've mastered the words, you can go on to try out the activities and games for that topic.

There's also a **Round-up** section to review all your new words and the **Answers** to all the activities to check yourself.

Follow this 4-step plan for maximum success:

1 Have a look at the key topic words with their pictures. Then tear out the flashcards and shuffle them. Put them Korean side up. Try to remember what the word means and turn the card over to check with the English. When you can do this, cover the pronunciation and try to say the word and remember the meaning by looking at the Korean script only.

2 Put the cards English side up and try to say the Korean word. Try the cards again each day both ways around. (When you can remember a card for 7 days in a row, you can file it!)

3 Try out the activities and games for each topic. This will reinforce your recognition of the key words.

4 After you have covered all the topics, you can try the activities in the **Round-up** section to test your knowledge of all the Korean words in the book. You can also try shuffling all the flashcards together to see how many you can remember.

This flexible and fun way of reading your first words in Korean should give you a head start whether you're learning at home or in a group.

◎ SCRIPTBREAKER

The purpose of this Scriptbreaker is to introduce you to the Korean script and how it is formed. You should not try to memorize the alphabet at this stage, nor try to write the letters yourself. Instead, have a quick look through this section and then move on to the topics, glancing back if you want to work out the letters in a particular word. Remember, though, that recognizing the whole shape of the word in an unfamiliar script is just as important as knowing how it is made up. Using this method you will have a much more instinctive recall of vocabulary and will gain the confidence to expand your knowledge in other directions.

The Korean script – more properly called the Hangul script – is not nearly as difficult as it might seem at first glance. Although Korean used to be written in Chinese characters (Hanja), these are now only rarely used and most everyday material is written in the Hangul alphabet developed in the 15th century by King Sejong.

The main difference between the Hangul scripts and most other scripts is that each syllable of a word is written together to form a square shape resembling a Chinese character – the only written shape familiar to 15th-century Koreans.

◎ The alphabet and syllables

There are 24 letters in the Hangul alphabet – 14 consonants and 10 vowels. These are listed on page 8 for your reference. It is better not to try and memorize them all immediately, but to understand the principles of how the alphabet works and then use the charts as you work your way through the book.

Unlike English, Korean words are generally spelled as they sound – although there are some exceptions to this rule. There are also no capital letters. The letters making up each syllable are written together to form a square shape. A syllable consists of:

- **consonant + vowel**, or sometimes
- **consonant + vowel + consonant**:

ㅈ *(j)* + ㅏ *(a)* = 자 *(ja)*

ㅅ *(s)* + ㅡ *(u)* = 스 *(su)*

ㄱ *(k)* + ㅣ *(ee)* = 기 *(kee)*

ㅁ *(m)* + ㅏ *(a)* + ㄹ *(l)* = 말 *(mal)*

Sometimes a consonant can be doubled (see **Pronunciation Tips**):

빠 (*ppa*)   싼 (*ssan*)

Note also that the letter ㅇ (*ng*) is silent when at the beginning of a syllable:

양 (*yang*)   오 (*aw*)   입 (*eep*)

Exactly how each combination of letters is written in a syllable (i.e. side-by-side, one on top of the other, etc.) is determined by the shape of the letters and convention. You don't have to know the conventions to read the syllables. A feeling for this will develop as you become more familiar with the script.

✔ Korean has 24 letters
✔ Letters making up a syllable are written together in a square shape
✔ There are no capital letters

◎ Making words

Some Korean words are made up of a single syllable, e.g.:

말 (*mal*) – horse   산 (*san*) – mountain

문 (*moon*) – door   등 (*tung*) – back

However, the majority of words are made of two or more syllables:

기차 (*keecha*) – train   손가락 (*sawn-garak*) – finger

사자 (*saja*) – lion   컴퓨터 (*kompyooto*) – computer

◎ Pronunciation tips

This exercise book has simplified some aspects of pronunciation in order to emphasize the basics. Don't worry at this stage about being precisely correct – the other letters in a word will help you to be understood.

Some Korean sounds are similar to their English equivalents, but others need special attention. The same letters can also be pronounced in a slightly different way depending on their position in a syllable, and this is reflected in the pronunciation given for the individual words.

Here are some points to note in particular:

ㅅ	pronounced as *s*, except when followed by *ee*, when it is pronounced as *sh*.
ㅎ	pronounced as *h* except at the end of a syllable, when it is pronounced *ng* as in "thing".
ㄹ	pronounced like a cross between an English "r" and "l". After an *m*, *n*, or *ng* sound, it is pronounced as *n*.
ㅏ	pronounced as a long "a" as in "arm".
ㅑ	pronounced as a long "ya" as in "yard".

Double consonants (see page 6) should be pronounced with more emphasis.

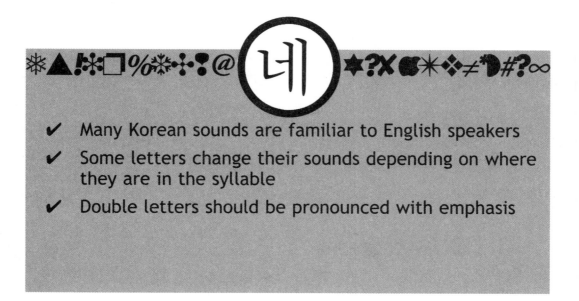

✔ Many Korean sounds are familiar to English speakers
✔ Some letters change their sounds depending on where they are in the syllable
✔ Double letters should be pronounced with emphasis

◎ Summary of the Korean Hangul alphabet

The tables below shows all the Korean letters. The shape of a letter will vary slightly depending on how it is combined with other letters in a syllable, but you should already recognize some of them, and as you move through the topics they will become more familiar to you.

Consonants

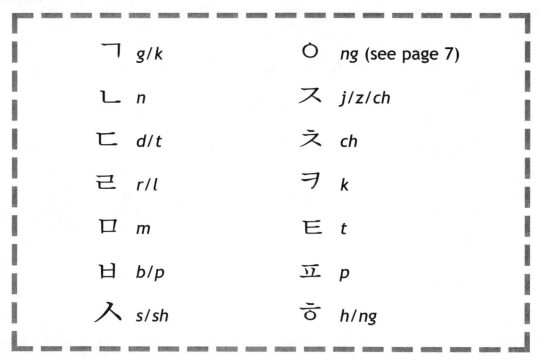

ㄱ	g/k	ㅇ	ng (see page 7)
ㄴ	n	ㅈ	j/z/ch
ㄷ	d/t	ㅊ	ch
ㄹ	r/l	ㅋ	k
ㅁ	m	ㅌ	t
ㅂ	b/p	ㅍ	p
ㅅ	s/sh	ㅎ	h/ng

Vowels/Vowel Combinations

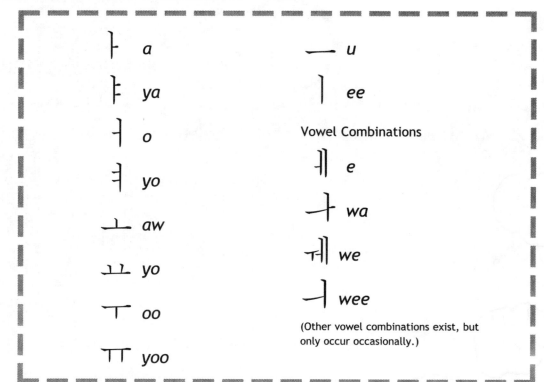

ㅏ	a	ㅡ	u
ㅑ	ya	ㅣ	ee
ㅓ	o		
ㅕ	yo	**Vowel Combinations**	
ㅗ	aw	ㅖ	e
ㅛ	yo	ㅘ	wa
ㅜ	oo	ㅞ	we
ㅠ	yoo	ㅟ	wee

(Other vowel combinations exist, but only occur occasionally.)

① Around the home

Look at the pictures of things you might find in a house.
Tear out the flashcards for this topic.
Follow steps 1 and 2 of the plan in the introduction.

창문
chang-moon

의자
wee-ja

탁자
takja

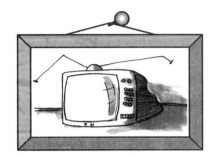

텔레비전
tel-lebeejon

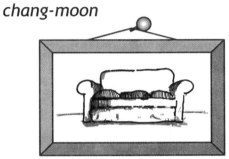

소파 *sawpa*

컴퓨터
kompyooto

전화기
chon-hwa-gee

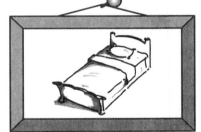

침대 *cheemde*

냉장고
neng-jang-gaw

찬장
chanzang

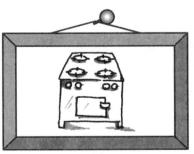

난로
nallaw

문
moon

9

◎ **M**atch the pictures with the words, as in the example.

소파
침대
창문
탁자
텔레비전
컴퓨터
전화기
의자

- -

◎ **N**ow match the Korean household words to the English.

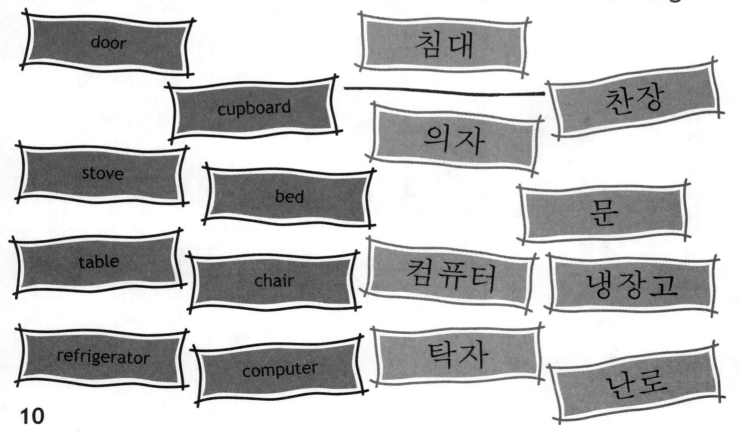

◎ **M**atch the words and their pronunciation.

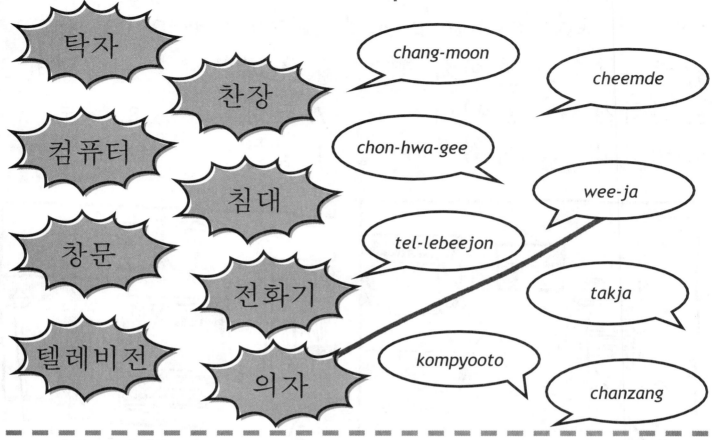

탁자

찬장

컴퓨터

침대

창문

전화기

텔레비전

의자

chang-moon

cheemde

chon-hwa-gee

wee-ja

tel-lebeejon

takja

kompyooto

chanzang

◎ **S**ee if you can find these words in the word square.
The words can run left to right, or top to bottom:

난로
침대
의자
냉장고
문
소파

내	일	카	부	락	스	여	미
토	침	미	냉	장	고	맙	안
문	다	히	사	한	요	안	침
합	소	합	근	난	로	금	퓨
큰	머	침	습	에	리	작	고
싼	녕	대	은	습	네	등	기
니	마	오	소	파	맙	탁	의
요	얼	끼	합	팔	고	근	자

11

○ **D**ecide where the household items should go. Then write the correct number in the picture, as in the example.

1. 탁자　　　2. 의자　　　3. 소파　　　4. 텔레비전
5. 전화기　　6. 침대　　　7. 찬장　　　8. 난로
9. 냉장고　　10. 컴퓨터　11. 창문　　12. 문

◎ **N**ow see if you can fill in the household word at the bottom of the page by choosing the correct Korean.

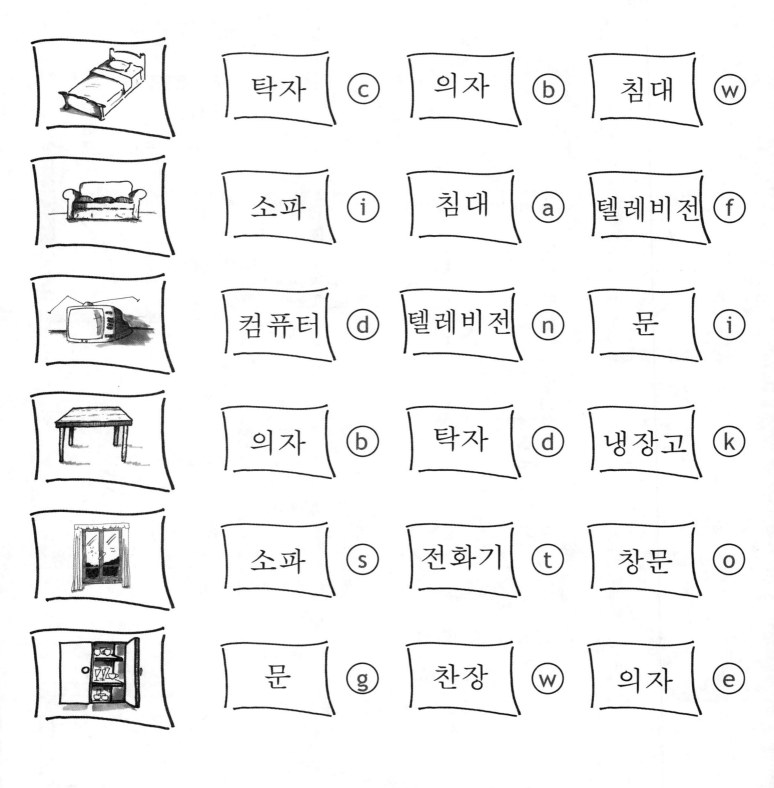

탁자 ⓒ 의자 ⓑ 침대 ⓦ

소파 ⓘ 침대 ⓐ 텔레비전 ⓕ

컴퓨터 ⓓ 텔레비전 ⓝ 문 ⓘ

의자 ⓑ 탁자 ⓓ 냉장고 ⓚ

소파 ⓢ 전화기 ⓣ 창문 ⓞ

문 ⓖ 찬장 ⓦ 의자 ⓔ

English word: ⓦ ◯ ◯ ◯ ◯ ◯

❷ CLOTHES

Look at the pictures of different clothes.
Tear out the flashcards for this topic.
Follow steps 1 and 2 of the plan in the introduction.

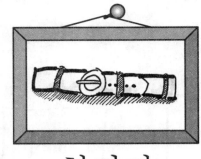

허리띠
horeettee

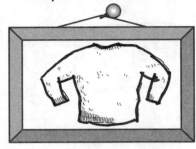

스웨터 *suweto*

반바지
panbajee

바지
pajee

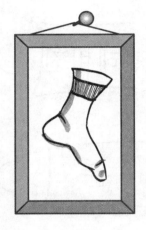

양말
yangmal

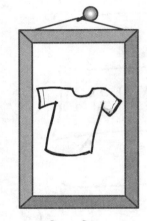

티셔츠
teesyochu

외투
weetoo

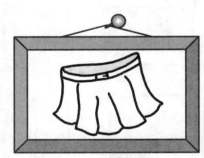

치마
cheema

드레스
turesu

모자 *mawja*

신발 *seenbal*

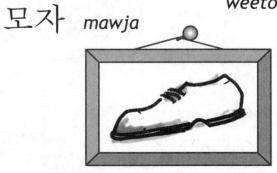

와이셔츠
wa-ee-syochu

◎ **M**atch the Korean words and their pronunciation.

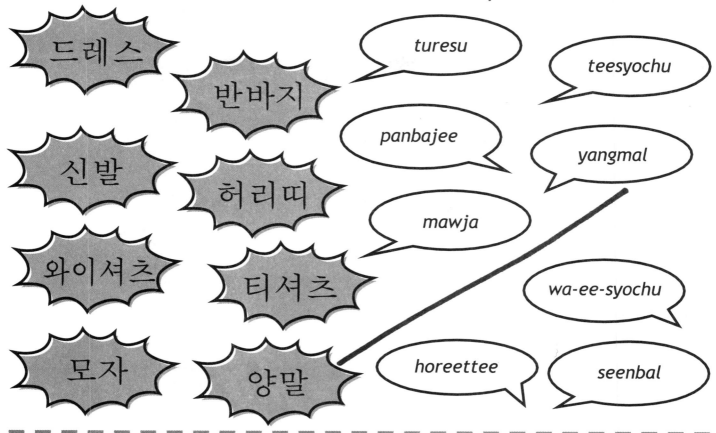

드레스

반바지

신발

허리띠

와이셔츠

티셔츠

모자

양말

turesu

teesyochu

panbajee

yangmal

mawja

wa-ee-syochu

horeettee

seenbal

◎ **S**ee if you can find these clothes in the word square.
The words can run left to right, or top to bottom:

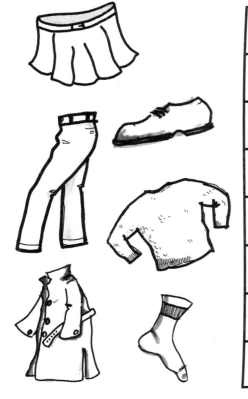

치	마	미	니	안	합	기	손
끼	침	토	이	판	외	맙	근
여	퓨	들	한	가	투	신	발
지	강	귀	스	부	한	침	귀
다	맙	입	웨	양	꿋	얼	말
고	습	대	터	락	장	바	깨
탁	양	말	금	요	사	지	마
스	미	히	에	녕	합	네	농

15

@ **N**ow match the Korean words, their pronunciation, and the English meaning, as in the example.

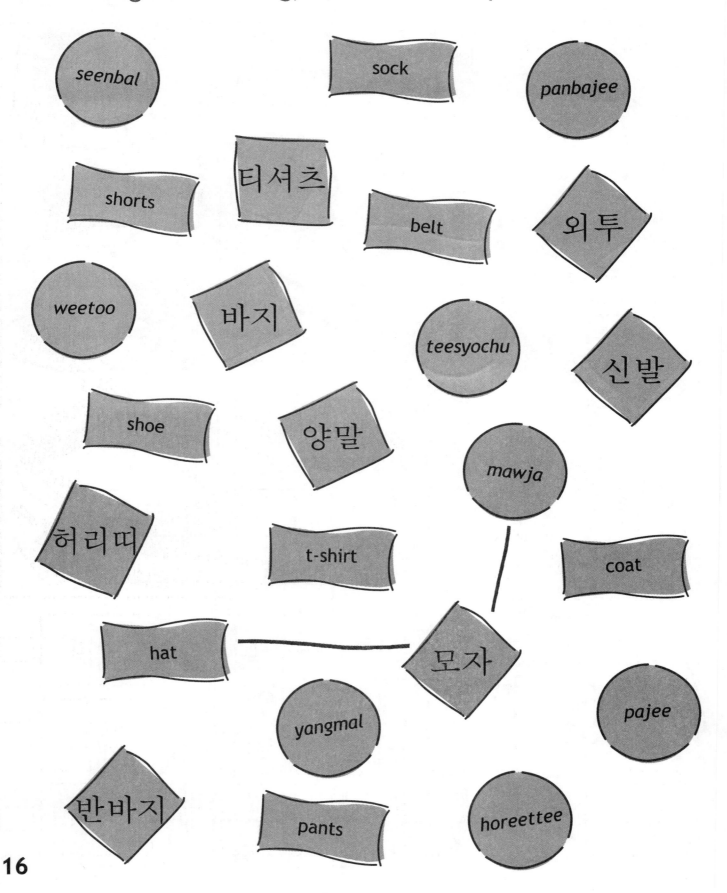

seenbal

sock

panbajee

shorts

티셔츠

belt

외투

weetoo

바지

teesyochu

신발

shoe

양말

mawja

허리띠

t-shirt

coat

hat

모자

pajee

yangmal

반바지

pants

horeettee

◎ **C**andy is going on vacation. Count how many of each type of clothing she is packing in her suitcase.

모자	2	외투	☐	허리띠	☐	신발	☐
바지	☐	반바지	☐	드레스	☐	양말	☐
치마	☐	티셔츠	☐	와이셔츠	☐	스웨터	☐

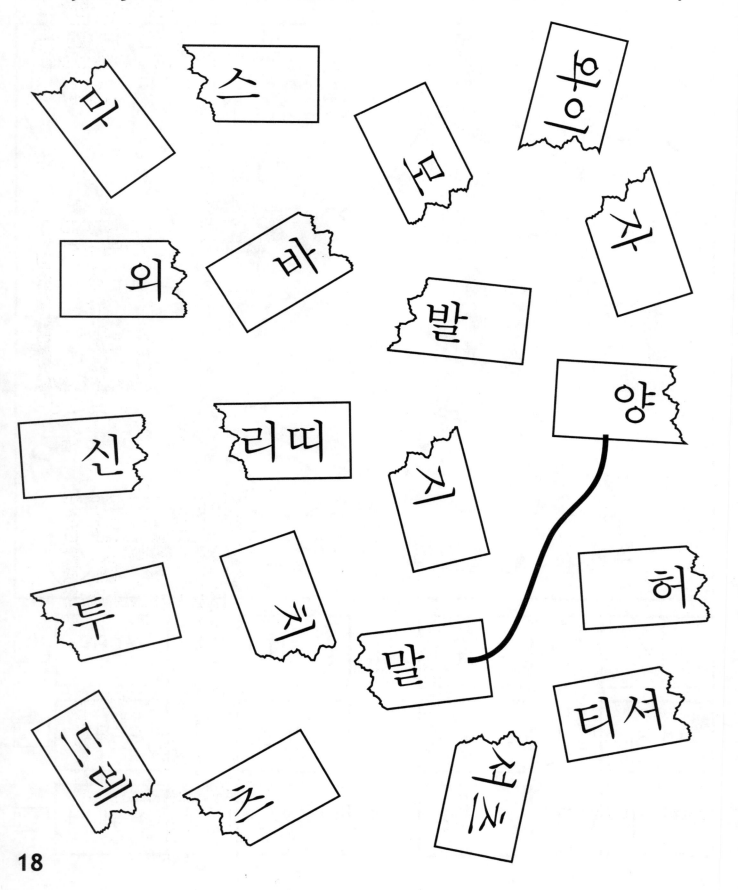

Someone has ripped up the Korean words for clothes. Can you join the two halves of the words, as the example?

스

우

파

외 바 모

신 리띠 발 자

양

투 지 지 허

말

트뢰 ㅉ 쵸ᅐ 티셔

③ AROUND TOWN

Look at the pictures of things you might see around town.
Tear out the flashcards for this topic.
Follow steps 1 and 2 of the plan in the introduction.

호텔 *hawtel*

버스 *posu*

집 *cheep*

자동차
cha-dawng-cha

영화관
yong-hwa-gwan

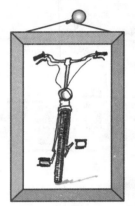

자전거
cha-jon-go

기차
keecha

택시 *teksee*

학교 *hak-gyo*

도로 *tawraw*

가게 *kage*

식당
seektang

19

Match the Korean words to their English equivalents.

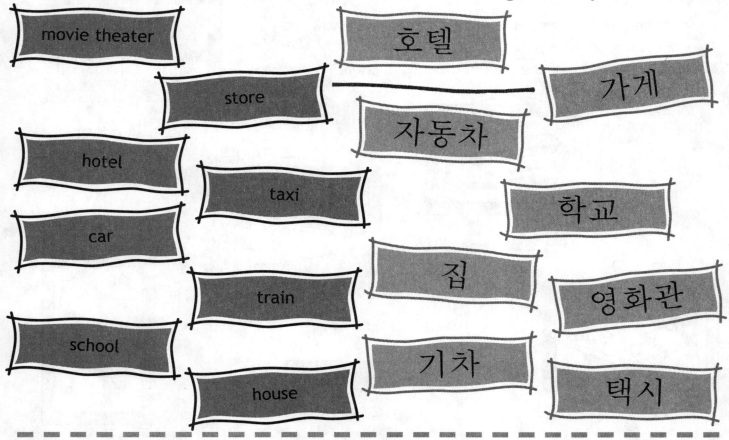

movie theater

store

호텔

가게

자동차

hotel

car

taxi

학교

집

영화관

school

train

기차

house

택시

Now put the English words in the same order as the Korean word chain, as in the example.

버스 — 집 — 도로 — 자전거 — 자동차 — 기차 — 택시

bicycle   taxi   house   bus   train   road   car

4 ___ ___ ___ ___ ___ ___

◎ **M**atch the words to the signs.

학교   자동차   자전거   호텔

식당   기차   버스   택시

Now choose the Korean word that matches the picture to fill in the English word at the bottom of the page.

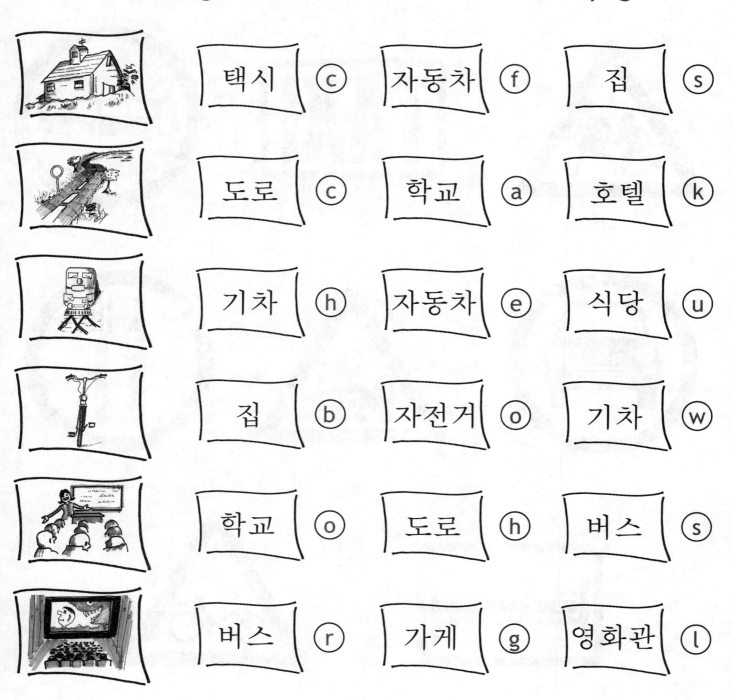

	택시 ⓒ	자동차 ⓕ	집 ⓢ
	도로 ⓒ	학교 ⓐ	호텔 ⓚ
	기차 ⓗ	자동차 ⓔ	식당 ⓤ
	집 ⓑ	자전거 ⓞ	기차 ⓦ
	학교 ⓞ	도로 ⓗ	버스 ⓢ
	버스 ⓡ	가게 ⓖ	영화관 ⓛ

Ⓔnglish word: ⓢ ◯ ◯ ◯ ◯ ◯

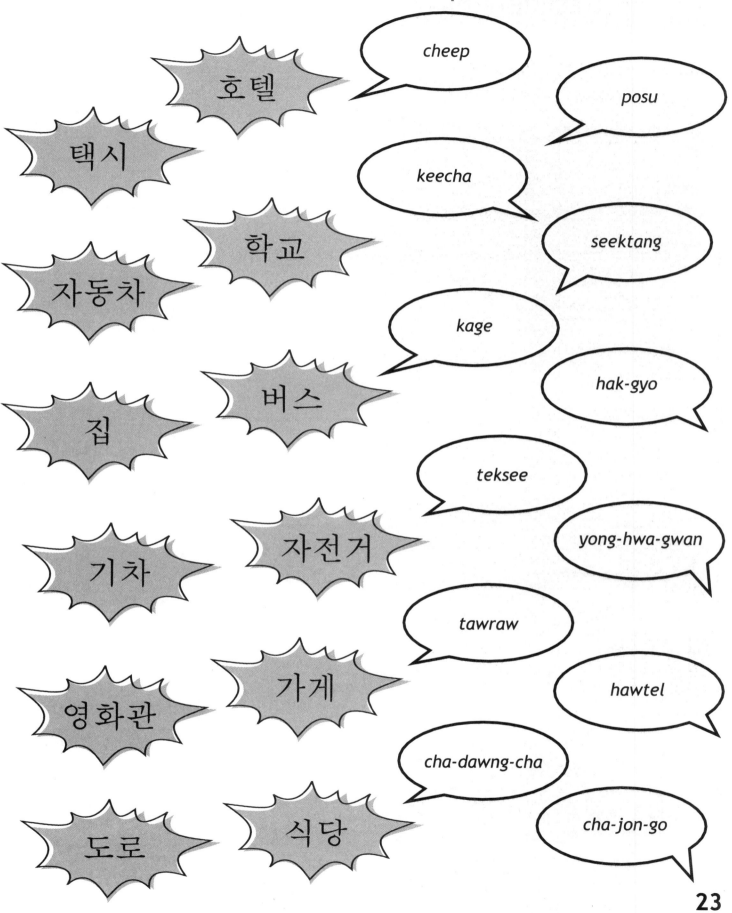

❹ COUNTRYSIDE

Look at the pictures of things you might find in the countryside.
Tear out the flashcards for this topic.
Follow steps 1 and 2 of the plan in the introduction.

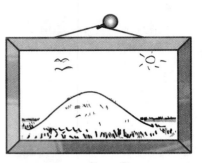

언덕
ondok

다리
taree

농장
nawng-jang

산
san

호수
hawsoo

나무
namoo

꽃
kkawt

강 *kang*

바다 *pada*

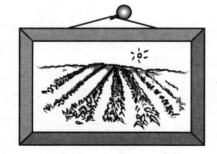

들판 *tulpan*

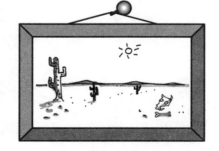

사막
samak

숲
soop

◎ **C**an you match all the countryside words to the pictures?

산

농장

바다

숲

사막

언덕

호수

다리

강

꽃

나무

들판

◎ **N**ow check (✔) the features you can find in this landscape.

다리 ✔   나무 ☐   사막 ☐   언덕 ☐

산 ☐   바다 ☐   들판 ☐   숲 ☐

호수 ☐   강 ☐   꽃 ☐   농장 ☐

◎ Match the Korean words and their pronunciation.

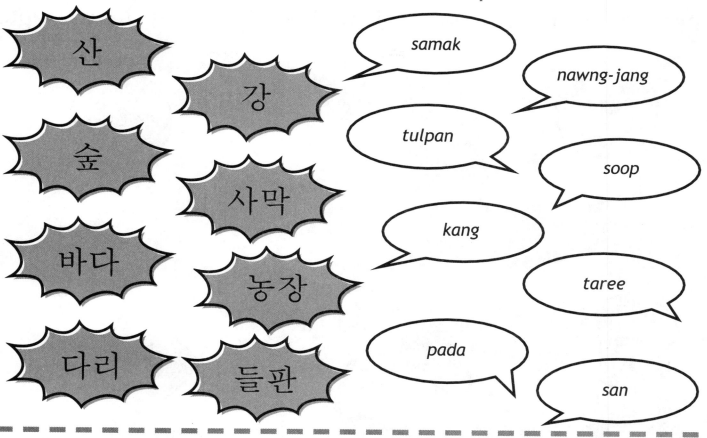

산

강 — samak

숲 — nawng-jang

사막 — tulpan

바다 — soop

농장 — kang

다리 — taree

들판 — pada

san

◎ See if you can find these words in the word square.
The words can run left to right, or top to bottom.

나무
농장
언덕
꽃
다리
호수

관	지	습	락	침	외	투	근
사	식	셔	언	덕	퓨	스	호
한	안	당	택	사	츠	얼	가
스	나	무	텔	이	손	팔	농
마	얼	화	와	양	한	시	장
에	호	맙	눈	영	여	다	녕
입	수	에	꽃	근	기	리	히
부	요	미	고	탁	합	금	네

◎ **F**inally, test yourself by joining the Korean words, their pronunciation, and the English meanings, as in the example.

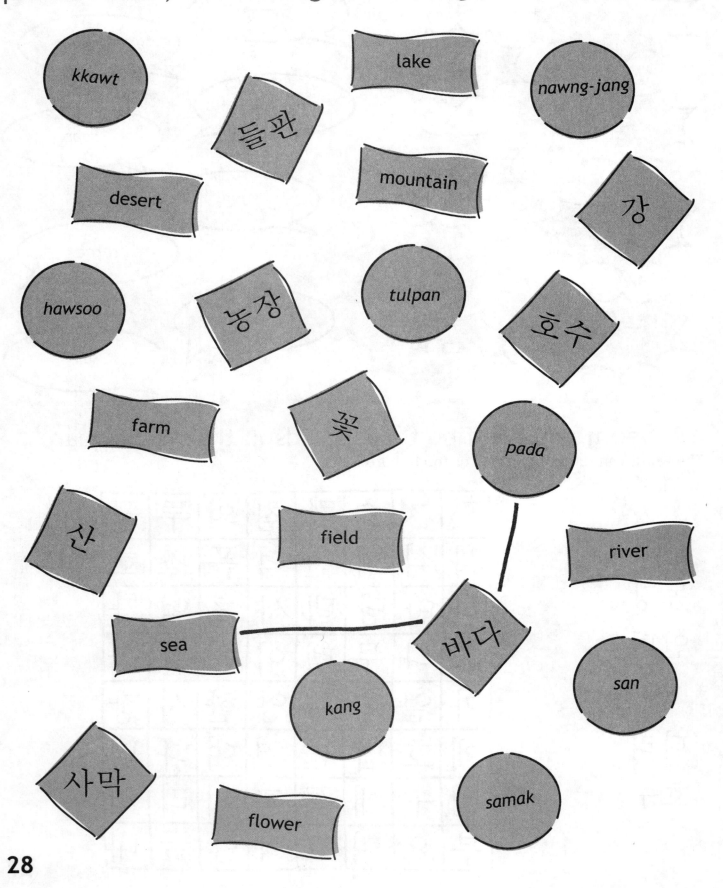

⑤ OPPOSITES

Look at the pictures.
Tear out the flashcards for this topic.
Follow steps 1 and 2 of the plan in the introduction.

더러운
toro-oon

깨끗한
kkekkutan

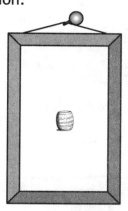

작은
chagun

큰 *kun*

싼 *ssan*

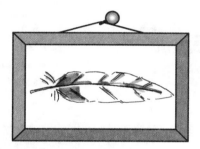

가벼운 *kabyo-oon*

느린 *nureen*

비싼 *pee-ssan*

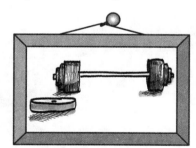

무거운 *moo-go-oon*

빠른 *pparun*

오래된 *awreden*

새로운 *seraw-oon*

Join the Korean words to their English equivalents.

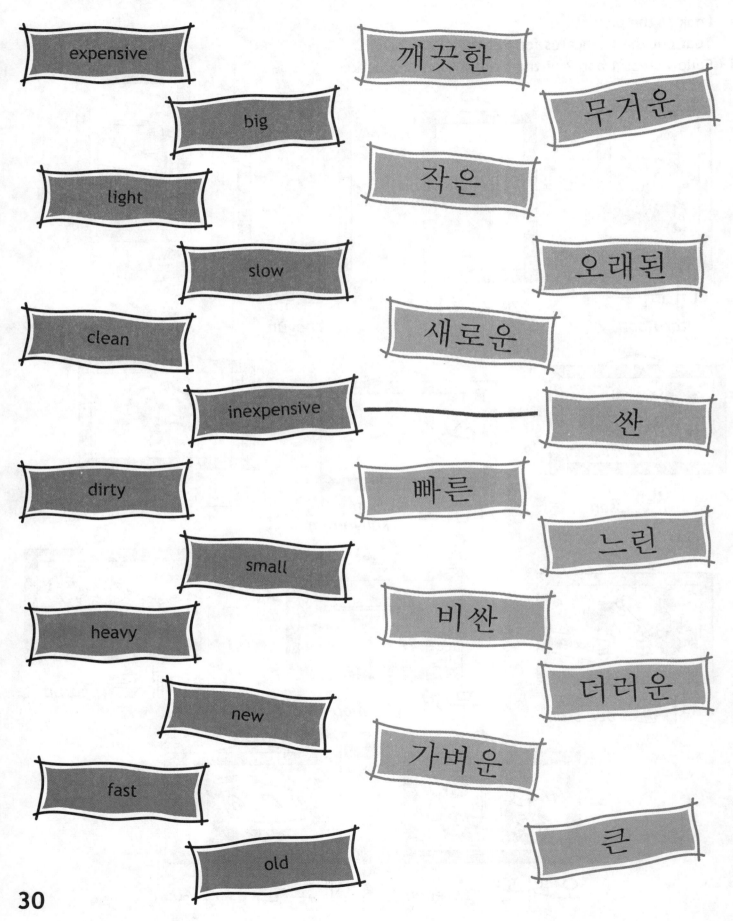

expensive

깨끗한

big

무거운

작은

light

오래된

slow

새로운

clean

inexpensive ——— 싼

dirty

빠른

느린

small

비싼

heavy

더러운

new

가벼운

fast

큰

old

30

🌀 **N**ow choose the Korean word that matches the picture to fill in the English word at the bottom of the page.

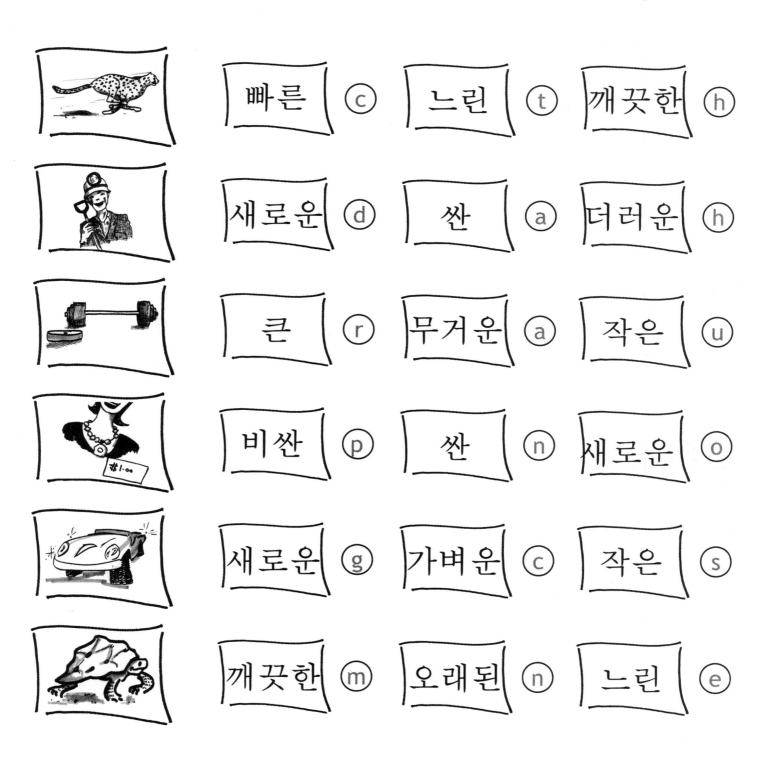

빠른 ⓒ   느린 ⓣ   깨끗한 ⓗ

새로운 ⓓ   싼 ⓐ   더러운 ⓗ

큰 ⓡ   무거운 ⓐ   작은 ⓤ

비싼 ⓟ   싼 ⓝ   새로운 ⓞ

새로운 ⓖ   가벼운 ⓒ   작은 ⓢ

깨끗한 ⓜ   오래된 ⓝ   느린 ⓔ

English word: ◯ ◯ ◯ ◯ ◯ ◯

Find the odd one out in these groups of words.

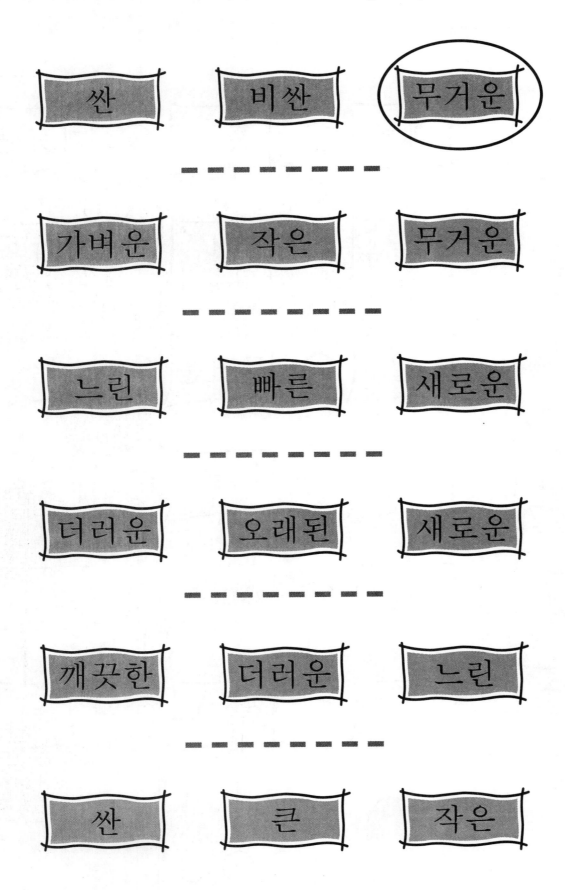

싼	비싼	(무거운)

| 가벼운 | 작은 | 무거운 |

| 느린 | 빠른 | 새로운 |

| 더러운 | 오래된 | 새로운 |

| 깨끗한 | 더러운 | 느린 |

| 싼 | 큰 | 작은 |

◎ **F**inally, join the English words to their Korean opposites, as in the example.

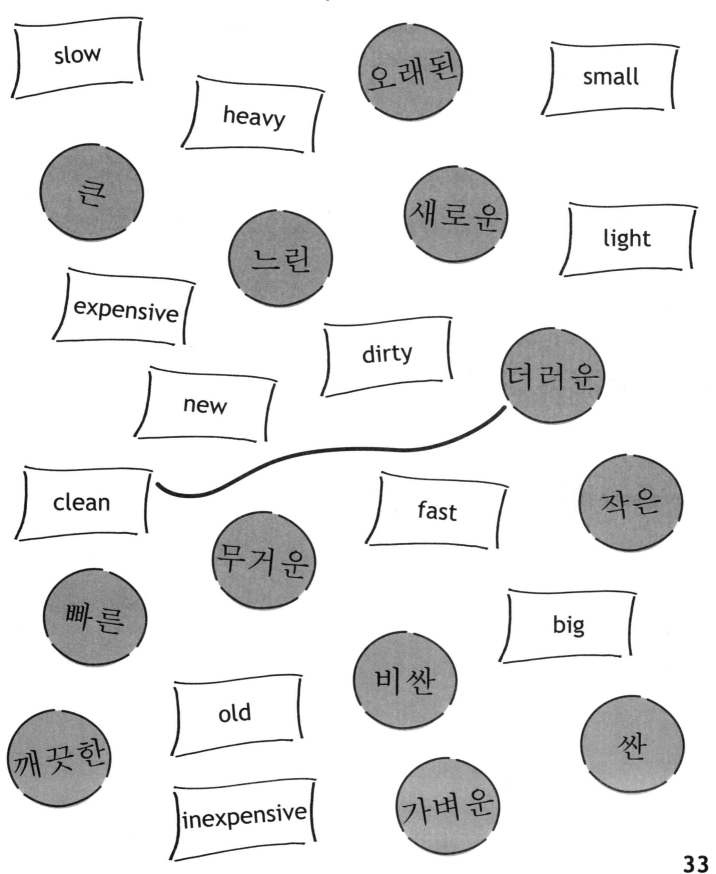

slow

오래된

small

heavy

큰

새로운

light

느린

expensive

dirty

더러운

new

clean

fast

작은

무거운

빠른

big

비싼

old

깨끗한

싼

inexpensive

가벼운

33

6 ANIMALS

Look at the pictures.
Tear out the flashcards for this topic.
Follow steps 1 and 2 of the plan in the introduction.

오리 *awree*

코끼리 *kaw-kkeeree*

고양이 *kaw-yang-ee*

개 *ke*

토끼 *taw-kkee*

원숭이 *won-soong-ee*

물고기 *moolgaw-gee*

양 *yang*

쥐 *chwee*

소 *saw*

말 *mal*

사자 *saja*

Match the animals to their associated pictures, as in the example.

토끼

말

원숭이

고양이

양

쥐

개

소

사자

물고기

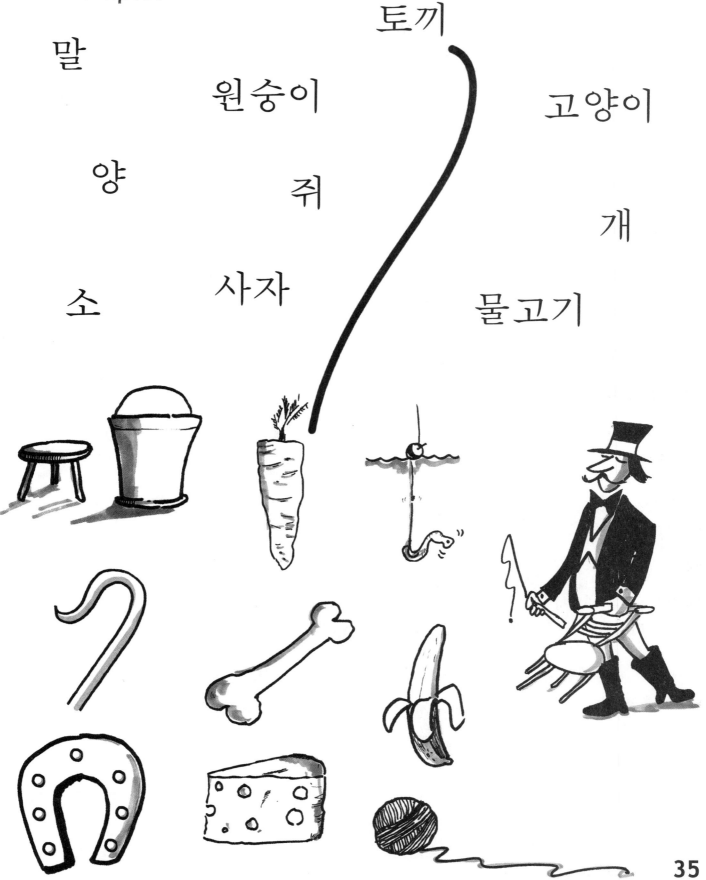

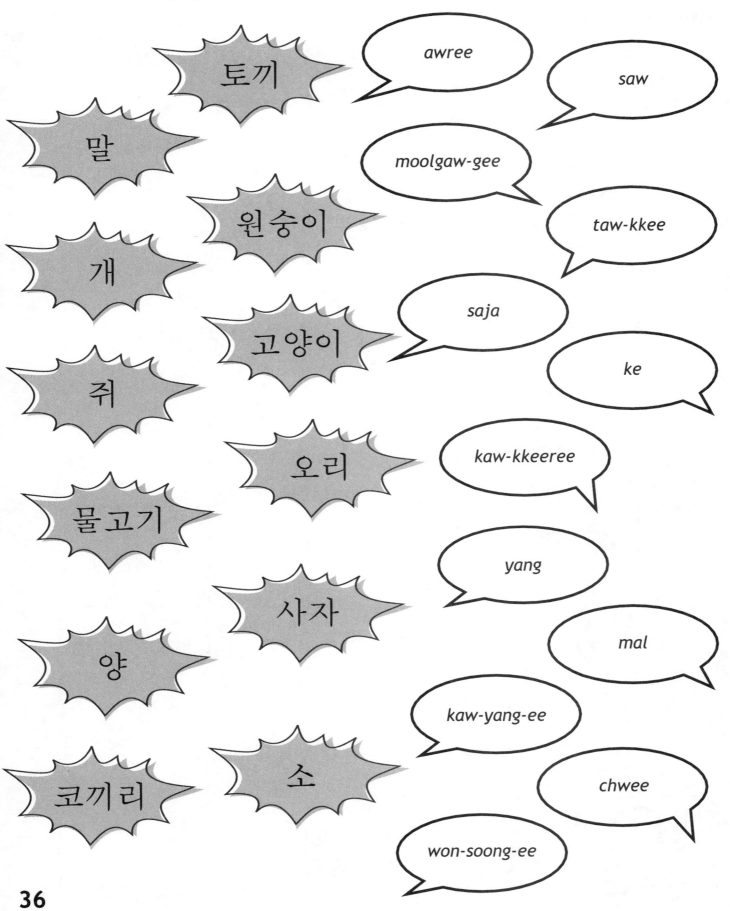

◎ **C**heck (✔) the animal words you can find in the word pile.

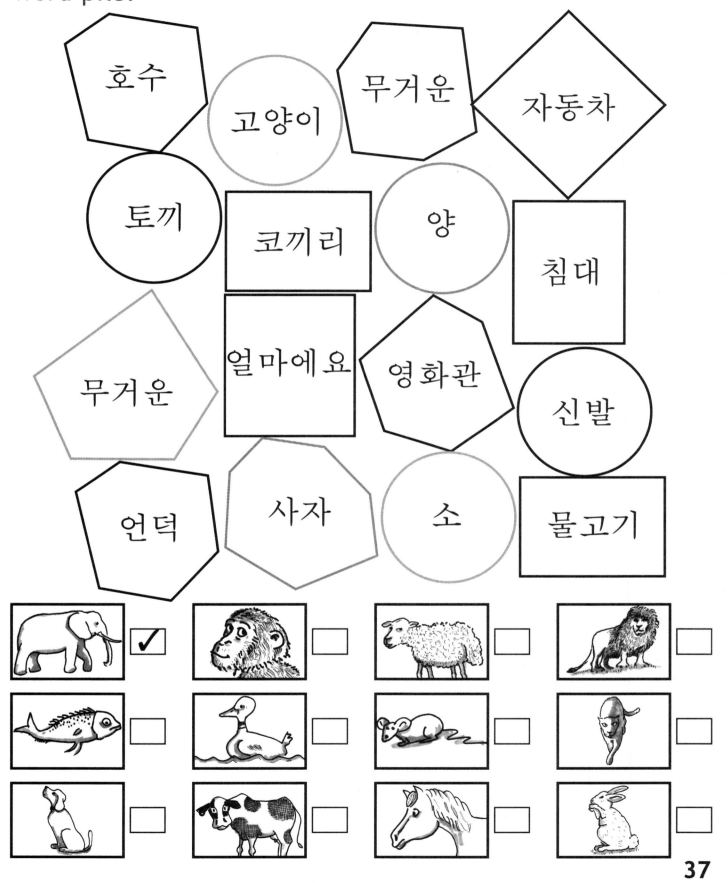

호수
고양이
무거운
자동차
토끼
코끼리
양
침대
무거운
얼마에요
영화관
신발
언덕
사자
소
물고기

Join the Korean animals to their English equivalents.

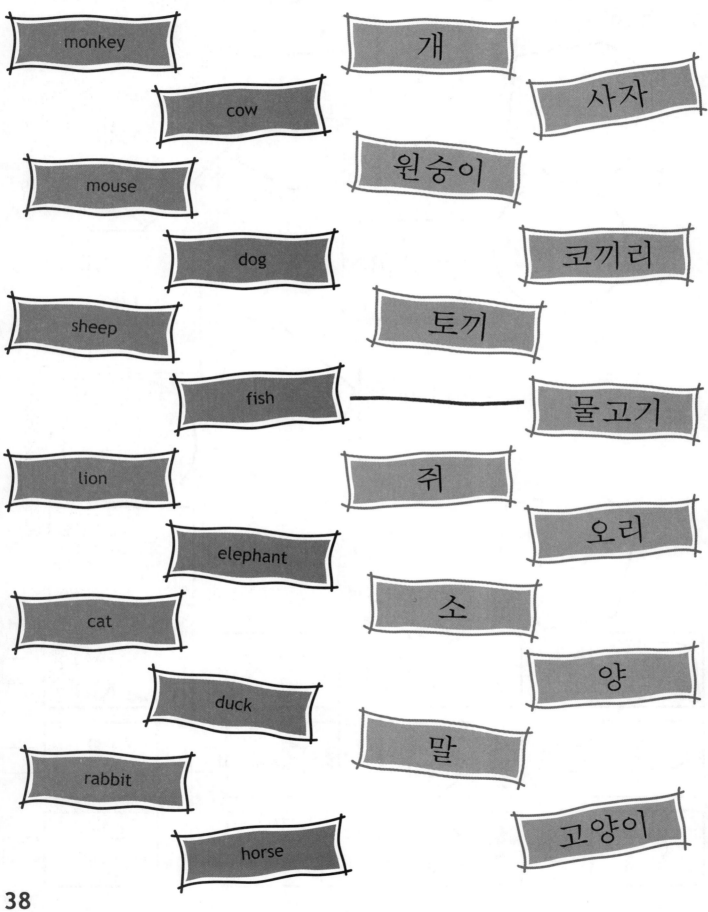

monkey	개
cow	사자
mouse	원숭이
dog	코끼리
sheep	토끼
fish	물고기
lion	쥐
elephant	오리
cat	소
duck	양
rabbit	말
horse	고양이

❼ PARTS OF THE BODY

Look at the pictures of parts of the body.
Tear out the flashcards for this topic.
Follow steps 1 and 2 of the plan in the introduction.

손가락
sawn-garak

팔 *pal*

눈 *noon*

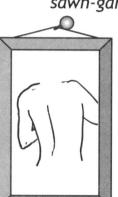

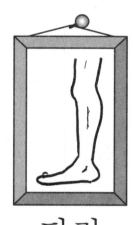

머리
moree

등 *tung*

손
sawn

다리
taree

배 *pe*

머리카락
moree-karak

귀
kwee

입 *eep*

코 *kaw*

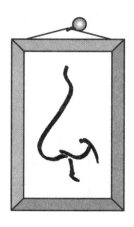

39

◎ **S**omeone has ripped up the Korean words for parts of the body. Can you join the two halves of the word again?

◎ **S**ee if you can find and circle six parts of the body in the word square, then draw them in the boxes below.

습	맙	입	고	합	다	미	안
기	여	얼	미	습	신	한	손
요	맙	마	안	다	리	탁	가
고	근	지	부	사	금	지	락
퓨	머	큰	습	안	맙	등	언
스	리	느	싼	배	에	니	여
기	카	꽃	얼	녕	히	네	침
미	락	린	발	덕	락	꽃	퓨

The words can run left to right, or top to bottom:

◎ **N**ow match the Korean to the pronunciation.

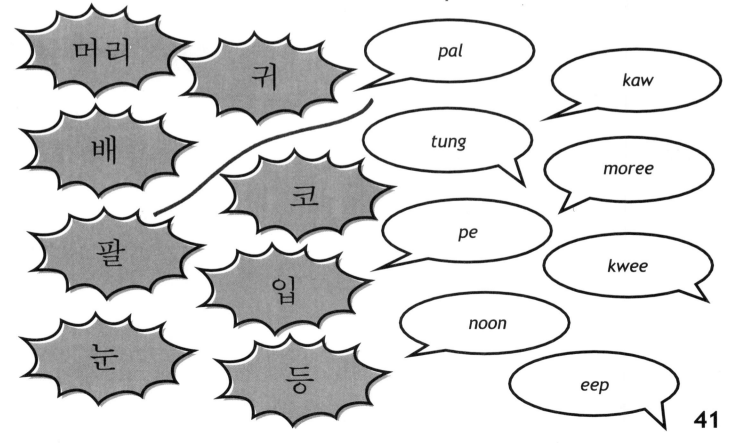

머리

귀

배

코

팔

입

눈

등

pal

kaw

tung

moree

pe

kwee

noon

eep

◎ **L**abel the body with the correct number, and write the pronunciation next to the words.

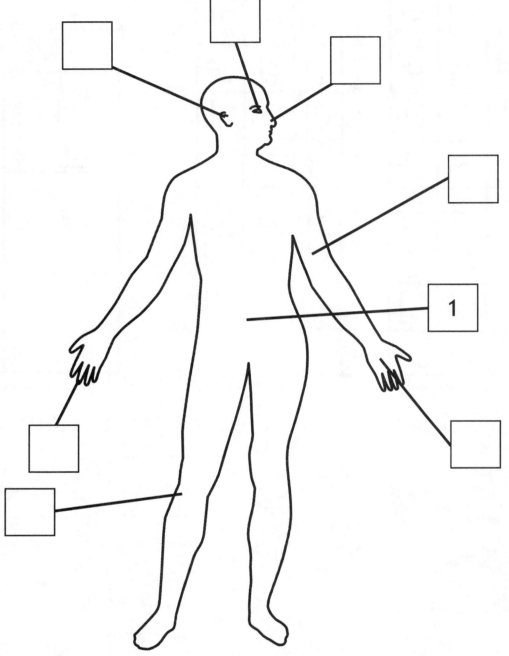

1 배 _pe_ _____   2 팔 _____

3 코 _____   4 손 _____

5 귀 _____   6 다리 _____

7 눈 _____   8 손가락 _____

◎ **F**inally, match the Korean words, their pronunciation, and the English meanings, as in the example.

sawn-garak

hair

taree

stomach

눈

hand

팔

pal

머리카락

sawn

배

back

손가락

손

arm

kwee

finger

ear

귀

tung

moree-karak

다리

leg

pe

43

⑧ USEFUL EXPRESSIONS

Look at the pictures.
Tear out the flashcards for this topic.
Follow steps 1 and 2 of the plan in the introduction.

어디? *odee*

아니요
aneeyo

네 *ne*

안녕하세요
an-nyong haseyo

안녕히 계세요
an-yong-hee keseyo

근사한
kunsahan

여기 *yo-gee*

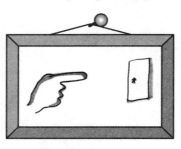

저기 *cho-gee*

지금 *chee-gum*

어제 *oje*

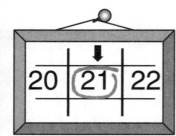

오늘 *awnul*

내일 *ne-eel*

얼마에요?
olma-eyo

미안합니다
meean-hamneeda

부탁합니다
pootak-hamneeda

고맙습니다
kawmap-sumneeda .

44

Match the Korean words to their English equivalents.

great

어제

yes

네

여기

yesterday

where?

근사한

today

here

부탁합니다

아니요

please

오늘

no

어디

Now match the Korean to the pronunciation.

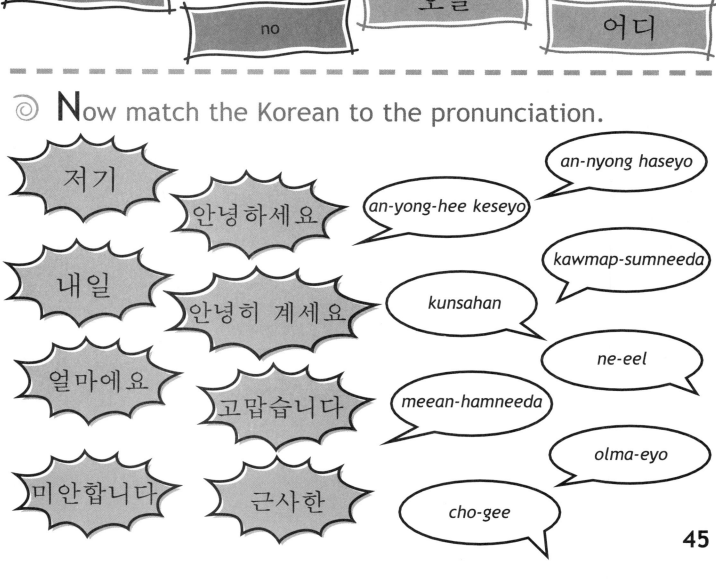

저기

안녕하세요

an-nyong haseyo

an-yong-hee keseyo

kawmap-sumneeda

내일

안녕히 계세요

kunsahan

ne-eel

얼마에요

고맙습니다

meean-hamneeda

olma-eyo

미안합니다

근사한

cho-gee

© **C**hoose the Korean word that matches the picture to fill in the English word at the bottom of the page.

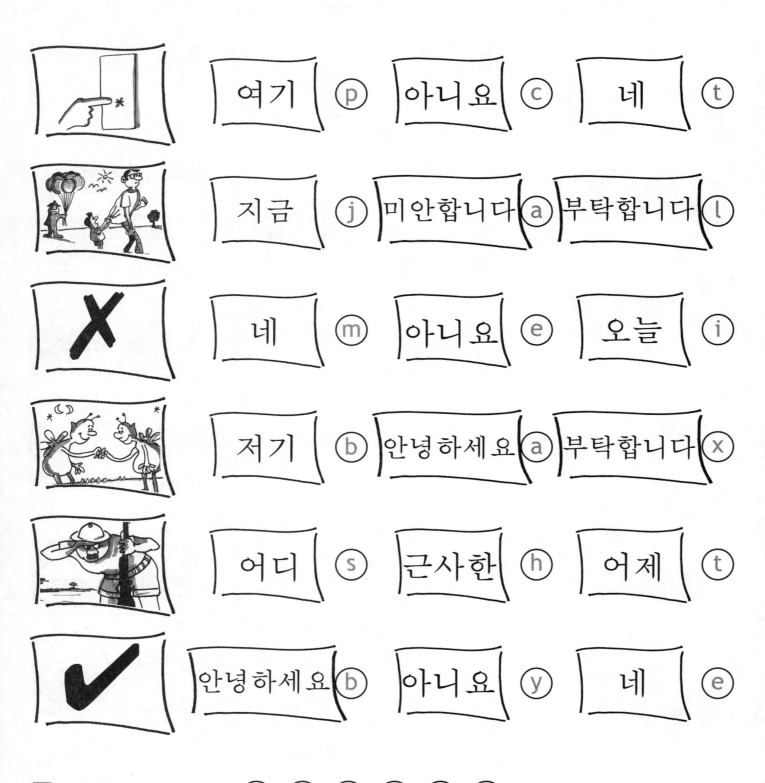

여기 (p)	아니요 (c)	네 (t)
지금 (j)	미안합니다 (a)	부탁합니다 (l)
네 (m)	아니요 (e)	오늘 (i)
저기 (b)	안녕하세요 (a)	부탁합니다 (x)
어디 (s)	근사한 (h)	어제 (t)
안녕하세요 (b)	아니요 (y)	네 (e)

English word: ⓟ ◯ ◯ ◯ ◯ ◯

What are these people saying? Write the correct number in each speech bubble, as in the example.

1. 안녕하세요   2. 부탁합니다   3. 네

4. 아니요   5. 여기   6. 미안합니다

7. 어디   8. 얼마에요

◎ **F**inally, match the Korean words, their pronunciation, and the English meanings, as in the example.

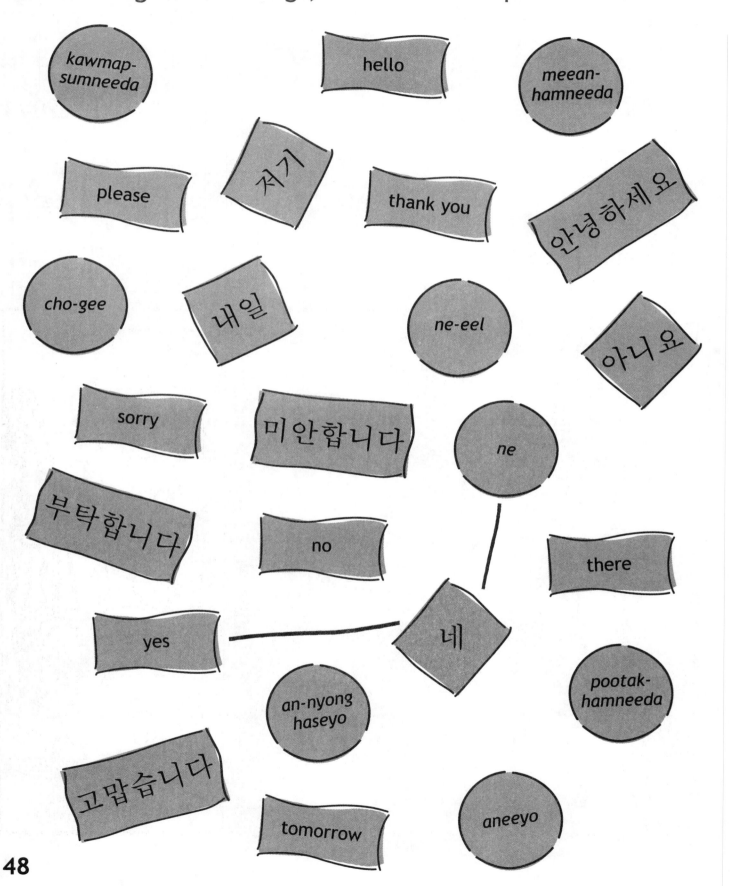

kawmap-sumneeda

hello

meean-hamneeda

please

저기

thank you

안녕하세요

cho-gee

내일

ne-eel

아니요

sorry

미안합니다

ne

부탁합니다

no

there

yes

네

an-nyong haseyo

pootak-hamneeda

고맙습니다

tomorrow

aneeyo

● ROUND-UP

This section is designed to review all the 100 words you have met in the different topics. It is a good idea to test yourself with your flashcards before trying this section.

◎ These ten objects are hidden in the picture. Can you find and circle them?

문	꽃	침대	외투	모자
자전거	의자	개	물고기	양말

See if you can remember all these words.

오늘
버스
빠른
코
사막
네
찬장
사자
드레스
싼
강
다리

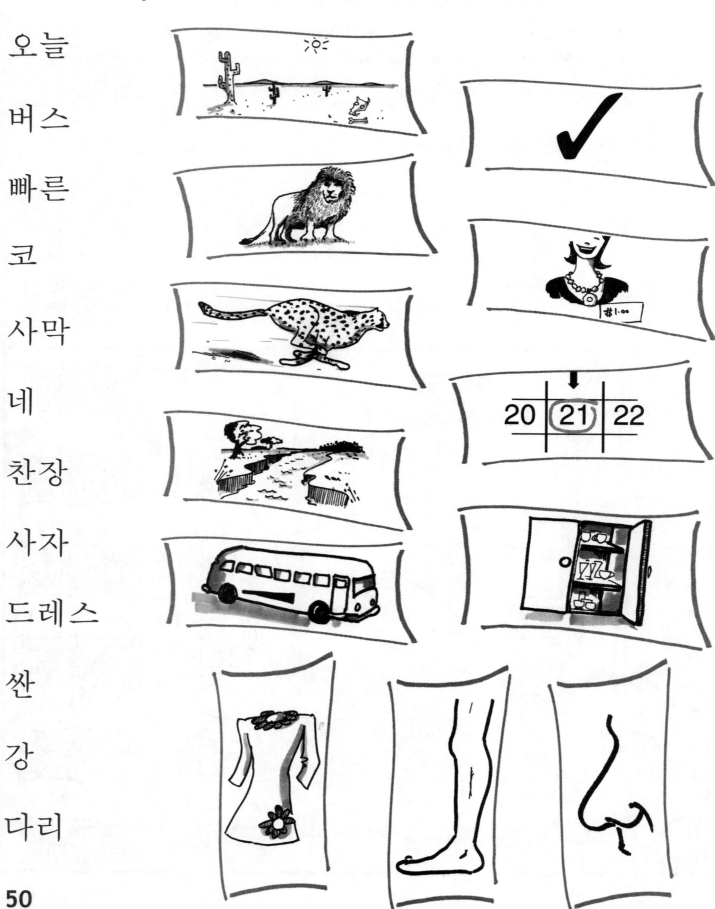

◎ **F**ind the odd one out in these groups of words and say why.

| 개 | 소 | 탁자 | 원숭이 |

Because it isn't an animal.

| 자동차 | 버스 | 기차 | 전화기 |

| 농장 | 외투 | 와이셔츠 | 치마 |

| 바다 | 호수 | 강 | 나무 |

| 비싼 | 더러운 | 깨끗한 | 영화관 |

| 토끼 | 고양이 | 물고기 | 사자 |

| 팔 | 소파 | 머리 | 배 |

| 부탁합니다 | 어제 | 내일 | 오늘 |

| 난로 | 침대 | 찬장 | 냉장고 |

◎ **L**ook at the objects below for 30 seconds.

◎ **C**over the picture and try to remember all the objects.
Circle the Korean words for those you remember.

꽃　　　신발　　　고맙습니다　　　문

자동차　　아니요　　여기

　　　　　　　　　산　　　외투　　기차

허리띠　　　　　　　　의자　　　　　말

　　　양말　　티셔츠　　　눈　　침대

반바지　　　택시　텔레비전　　　원숭이

Now match the Korean words, their pronunciation, and the English meanings, as in the example.

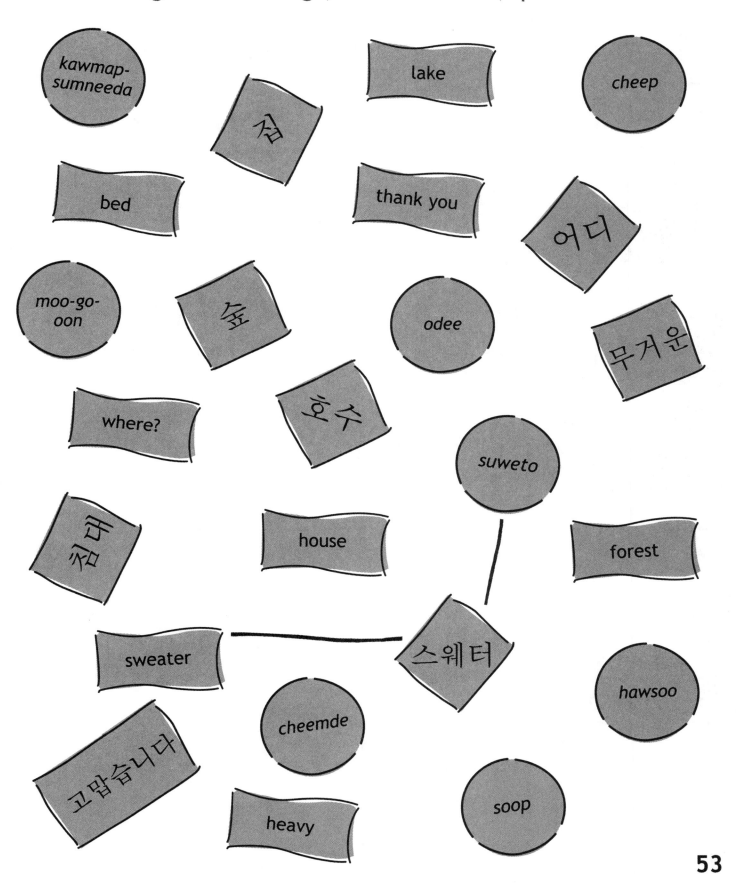

kawmap-sumneeda

lake

cheep

침

bed

thank you

어디

moo-go-oon

숲

odee

무거운

where?

호수

suweto

침대

house

forest

sweater

스웨터

hawsoo

고맙습니다

cheemde

heavy

soop

Fill in the English phrase at the bottom of the page.

소파 (w)	택시 (g)	귀 (t)
외투 (o)	더러운 (a)	다리 (e)
네 (m)	얼마에요 (l)	오늘 (i)
소 (b)	창문 (l)	식당 (h)
어디 (e)	입 (a)	개 (d)
눈 (o)	탁자 (p)	안녕하세요 (v)
언덕 (n)	아니요 (y)	호텔 (r)
토끼 (n)	도로 (e)	난로 (s)

54   English phrase: (w) ◯ ◯ ◯   ◯ ◯ ◯ ◯ !

Look at the two pictures and check (✔) the objects that are different in Picture B.

Picture A

Picture B

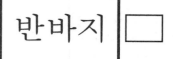 반바지 ☐

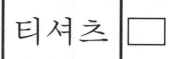 티셔츠 ☐

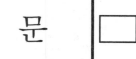 문 ☐

 고양이 ☐

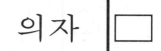 의자 ☐

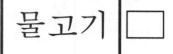 물고기 ☐

 양말 ☐

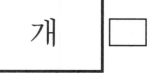 개 ☐

55

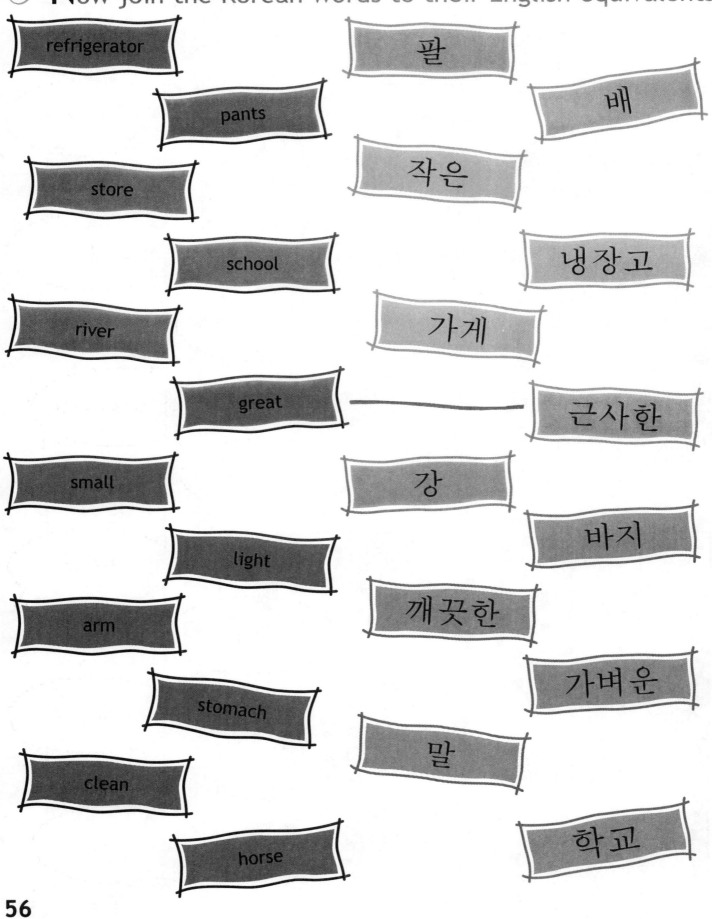

Now join the Korean words to their English equivalents.

refrigerator

팔

pants

배

store

작은

school

냉장고

river

가게

great

근사한

small

강

light

바지

arm

깨끗한

stomach

가벼운

clean

말

horse

학교

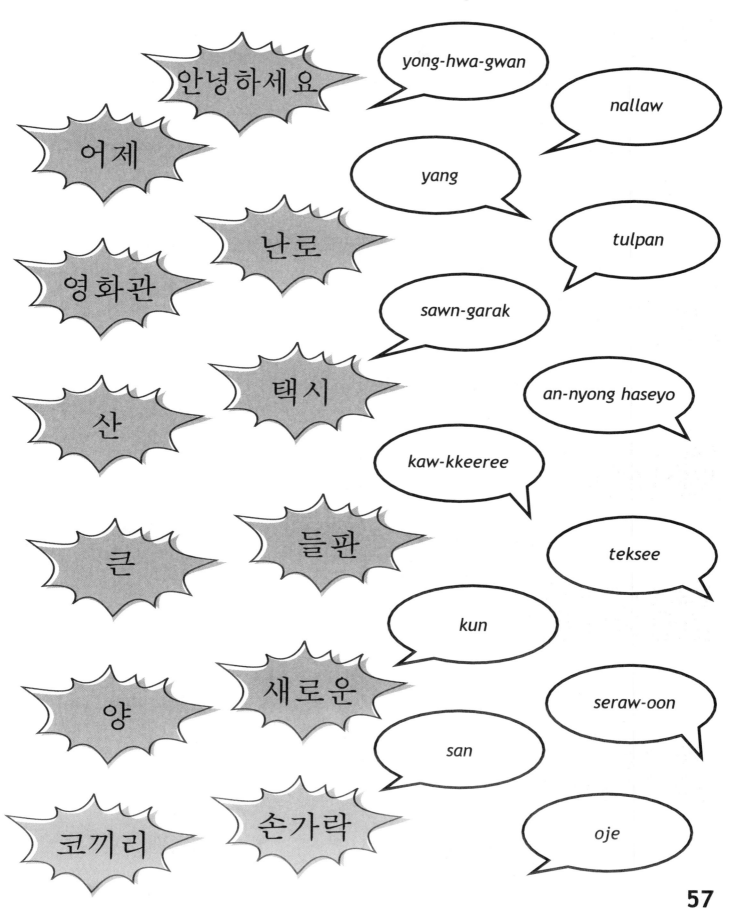

⊚ Snake game.

● You will need a die and counter(s). You can challenge yourself to reach the finish or play with someone else. You have to throw the exact number to finish.

● Throw the die and move forward that number of spaces. When you land on a word you must pronounce it and say what it means in English. If you can't, you have to go back to the square you came from.

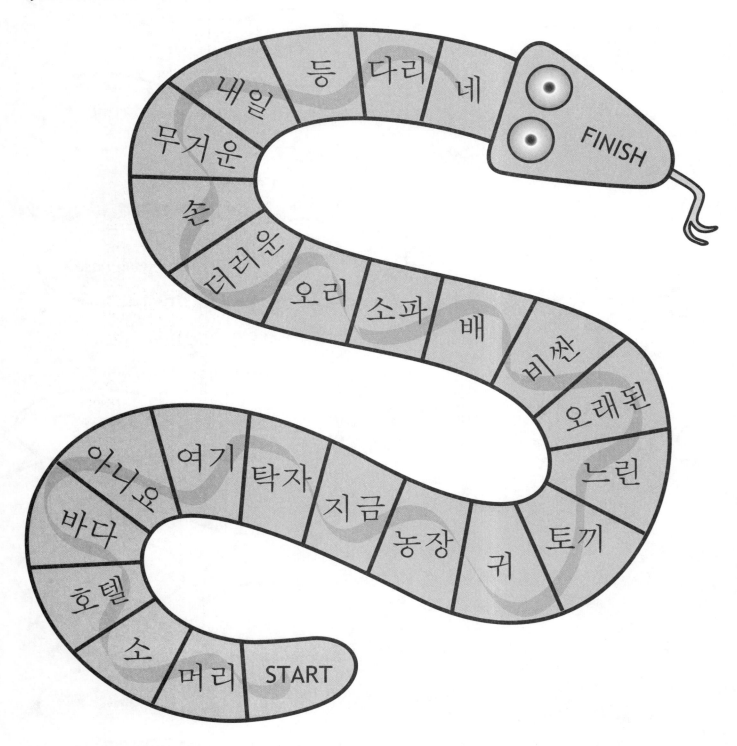

⊚ Answers

❶ AROUND THE HOME

Page 10 (top)

See page 9 for correct picture.

Page 10 (bottom)

door	문
cupboard	찬장
stove	난로
bed	침대
table	탁자
chair	의자
refrigerator	냉장고
computer	컴퓨터

Page 11 (top)

탁자	*takja*
찬장	*chanzang*
컴퓨터	*kompyooto*
침대	*cheemde*
창문	*chang-moon*
전화기	*chon-hwa-gee*
텔레비	*tel-lebeejon*
의자	*u-ee-ja*

Page 11 (bottom)

Page 12

Page 13

English word: window

❷ CLOTHES

Page 15 (top)

드레스	*turesu*
반바지	*panbajee*
신발	*seenbal*
허리띠	*horeetee*
와이셔츠	*wa-ee-syochu*
티셔츠	*teesyochu*
모자	*mawja*
양말	*yangmal*

Page 15 (bottom)

Page 16

hat	모자	*mawja*
shoe	신발	*seenbal*
sock	양말	*yangmal*
shorts	반바지	*panbajee*
t-shirt	티셔츠	*teesyochu*
belt	허리띠	*horeettee*
coat	외투	*weetoo*
pants	바지	*pajee*

Page 17

모자 (hat)	2
외투 (coat)	0
허리띠 (belt)	2
신발 (shoe)	2 (1 pair)
바지 (pants)	0
반바지 (shorts)	2
드레스 (dress)	1
양말 (sock)	6 (3 pairs)
치마 (skirt)	1
티셔츠 (t-shirt)	3
와이셔츠 (shirt)	0
스웨터 (sweater)	1

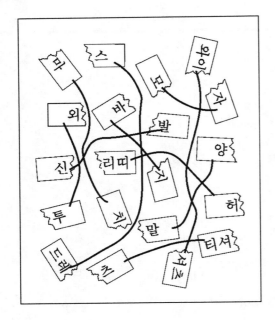

❸ AROUND TOWN

Page 20 (top)

movie theater	영화관
store	가게
hotel	호텔
taxi	택시
car	자동차
train	기차
school	학교
house	집

Page 20 (bottom)

bicycle	4
taxi	7
house	2
bus	1
train	6
road	3
car	5

Page 21

학교　택시　버스

자동차　기차　식당

호텔　자전거

English word: school

Page 23

버스	*posu*
택시	*teksee*
학교	*hak-gyo*
자동차	*cha-dawng-cha*
호텔	*hawtel*
집	*cheep*
자전거	*cha-jon-go*
기차	*keecha*
가게	*kage*
영화관	*yong-hwa-gwan*
식당	*seektang*
도로	*tawraw*

❹ COUNTRYSIDE

Page 25

See page 24 for correct picture.

Page 26

다리 ✔	나무 ✔	사막 ✘	언덕 ✘
산 ✔	바다 ✘	들판 ✔	숲 ✘
호수 ✘	강 ✔	꽃 ✔	농장 ✔

Page 27 (top)

산	*san*
강	*kang*
숲	*soop*
사막	*samak*
바다	*pada*
농장	*nawng-jang*
다리	*taree*
들판	*tulpan*

Page 27 (bottom)

관	지	습	락	침	외	투	근
사	식	셔	언	덕	퓨	스	호
한	안	당	택	사	츠	얼	가
스	나	무	텔	이	손	팔	농
마	얼	화	와	양	한	시	장
에	호	맙	눈	영	여	다	녕
입	수	에	꽃	근	기	리	히
부	요	미	고	탁	합	금	네

Page 28

sea	바다	*pada*
lake	호수	*hawsoo*
desert	사막	*samak*
farm	농장	*nawng-jang*
flower	꽃	*kkawt*
mountain	산	*san*
river	강	*kang*
field	들판	*tulpan*

❺ OPPOSITES

Page 30

expensive	비싼
	큰 big
light	가벼운
slow	느린
clean	깨끗한
inexpensive	싼
dirty	더러운
small	작은
heavy	무거운
new	새로운
fast	빠른
old	오래된

Page 31
English word: change

Page 32
Odd one outs are those which are not opposites:
무거운
작은
새로운
더러운
느린
싼

Page 33

old	새로운
big	작은
new	오래된
slow	빠른
dirty	깨끗한
small	큰
heavy	가벼운
clean	더러운
light	무거운
inexpensive	싼
expensive	비싼
fast	느린

❻ ANIMALS

Page 35

소   토끼   물고기   사자

양   개   원숭이

말   쥐   고양이

Page 36

토끼	*taw-kkee*
말	*mal*
원숭이	*won-soong-ee*
개	*ke*
고양이	*kaw-yang-ee*
쥐	*chwee*
오리	*awree*
물고기	*moolgaw-gee*
사자	*saja*
양	*yang*
소	*saw*
코끼리	*kaw-kkeeree*

Page 37

elephant	✔	mouse	✘
monkey	✘	cat	✔
sheep	✔	dog	✘
lion	✔	cow	✔
fish	✔	horse	✘
duck	✘	rabbit	✔

Page 38

monkey	원숭이
cow	소
mouse	쥐
dog	개
sheep	양
fish	물고기
lion	사자
elephant	코끼리
cat	고양이
duck	오리
rabbit	토끼
horse	말

❼ PARTS OF THE BODY

Page 40

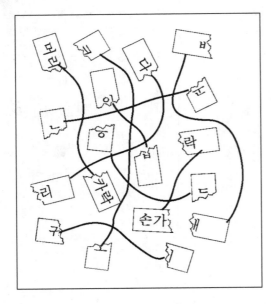

Page 41 (top)

You should have also drawn pictures of:

leg; mouth; back; finger; stomach; hair

Page 41 (bottom)

머리	*moree*
귀	*kwee*
배	*pe*
코	*kaw*
팔	*pal*
입	*eep*
눈	*noon*
등	*tung*

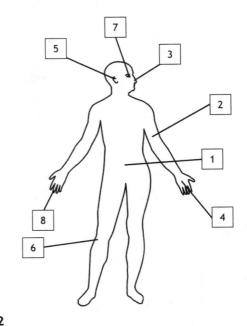

Page 42

1. 배	*pe*
2. 팔	*pal*
3. 코	*kaw*
4. 손	*sawn*
5. 귀	*kwee*
6. 다리	*taree*
7. 눈	*noon*
8. 손가락	*sawn-garak*

Page 43

ear	귀	*kwee*
hair	머리카락	*moree-karak*
hand	손	*sawn*
stomach	배	*pe*
arm	팔	*pal*
back	등	*tung*
finger	손가락	*sawn-garak*
leg	다리	*taree*

❽ USEFUL EXPRESSIONS

Page 45 (top)

great	근사한
yes	네
yesterday	어제
where?	어디
today	오늘
here	여기
please	부탁합니다
no	아니요

Page 45 (bottom)

저기	cho-gee
안녕하세요	an-nyong haseyo
내일	ne-eel
안녕히 계세요	an-yong-hee keseyo
얼마에요	olma-eyo
고맙습니다	kawmap-sumneeda
미안합니다	meean-hamneeda
근사한	kunsahan

Page 46

English word: please

Page 47

Page 48

yes	네	ne
hello	안녕하세요	an-nyong haseyo
no	아니요	aneeyo
sorry	미안합니다	meean-hamneeda
please	부탁합니다	pootak-hamneeda
there	저기	cho-gee
thank you	고맙습니다	kawmap-sumneeda
tomorrow	내일	ne-eel

● ROUND-UP

Page 49

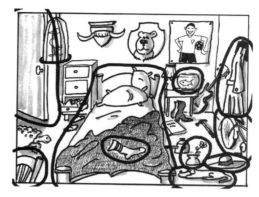

Page 50

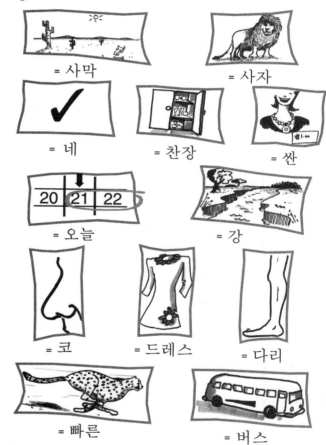

= 사막   = 사자

= 네   = 찬장   = 싼

= 오늘   = 강

= 코   = 드레스   = 다리

= 빠른   = 버스

Page 51

탁자 (Because it isn't an animal.)

전화기 (Because it isn't a means of transportation.)

농장 (Because it isn't an item of clothing.)

나무 (Because it isn't connected with water.)

영화관 (Because it isn't a descriptive word.)

물고기 (Because it lives in water/doesn't have legs.)

소파 (Because it isn't a part of the body.)

부탁합니다 (Because it isn't an expression of time.)

침대 (Because you wouldn't find it in the kitchen.)

Page 52

Words that appear in the picture:

티셔츠
자동차
꽃
신발
기차
원숭이
텔레비전
의자
허리띠
반바지

Page 53

sweater	스웨터	*suweto*
lake	호수	*hawsoo*
thank you	고맙습니다	*kawmap-sumneeda*
bed	침대	*cheemde*
house	집	*cheep*
forest	숲	*soop*
where?	어디	*odee*
heavy	무거운	*moo-go-oon*

Page 54

English phrase: well done!

Page 55

반바지	✔ (shade)
티셔츠	✘
문	✔ (handle)
고양이	✘
의자	✔ (back)
물고기	✔ (direction)
양말	✔ (pattern)
개	✘

Page 56

refrigerator	냉장고
pants	바지
store	가게
school	학교
river	강
great	근사한
small	작은
light	가벼운
arm	팔
stomach	배
clean	깨끗한
horse	말

Page 57

안녕하세요	*an-nyong haseyo*
어제	*oje*
난로	*nallaw*
영화관	*yong-hwa-gwan*
택시	*teksee*
산	*san*
들판	*tulpan*
큰	*kun*
새로운	*seraw-oon*
양	*yang*
손가락	*sawn-garak*
코끼리	*kaw-kkeeree*

Page 58

Here are the English equivalents of the word, in order from START to FINISH:

head	*moree*	old	*awreden*
cow	*saw*	expensive	*pee-ssan*
hotel	*hawtel*	stomach	*pe*
sea	*pada*	sofa	*sawpa*
no	*aneeyo*	duck	*awree*
here	*yo-gee*	dirty	*toro-oon*
table	*takja*	hand	*sawn*
now	*chee-gum*	heavy	*moo-go-oon*
farm	*nawng-jang*	tomorrow	*ne-eel*
ear	*kwee*	back	*tung*
rabbit	*taw-kkee*	leg	*taree*
slow	*nureen*	yes	*ne*

컴퓨터

kompyooto

창문

chang-moon

탁자

takja

찬장

chanzang

냉장고

neng-jang-gaw

의자

wee-ja

소파

sawpa

난로

nallaw

문

moon

침대

cheemde

전화기

chon-hwa-gee

텔레비전

tel-lebeejon

window	computer
cupboard	table
chair	refrigerator
stove	sofa
bed	door
television	telephone

허리띠

horeettee

외투

weetoo

치마

cheema

모자

mawja

티셔츠

teesyochu

신발

seenbal

스웨터

suweto

와이셔츠

wa-ee-syochu

반바지

panbajee

양말

yangmal

바지

pajee

드레스

turesu

coat	belt
hat	skirt
shoe	t-shirt
shirt	sweater
sock	shorts
dress	pants

학교

hak-gyo

자동차

cha-dawng-cha

도로

tawraw

영화관

yong-hwa-gwan

호텔

hawtel

가게

kage

택시

teksee

자전거

cha-jon-go

식당

seektang

버스

posu

기차

keecha

집

cheep

car	school
movie theater	road
store	hotel
bicycle	taxi
bus	restaurant
house	train

호수

hawsoo

숲

soop

언덕

ondok

바다

pada

산

san

나무

namoo

사막

samak

꽃

kkawt

다리

taree

강

kang

농장

nawng-jang

들판

tulpan

forest	lake
sea	hill
tree	mountain
flower	desert
river	bridge
field	farm

무거운

moo-go-oon

가벼운

kabyo-oon

큰

kun

작은

chagun

오래된

awreden

새로운

seraw-oon

빠른

pparun

느린

nureen

깨끗한

kkekkutan

더러운

toro-oon

싼

ssan

비싼

pee-ssan

light	heavy
small	big
new	old
slow	fast
dirty	clean
expensive	inexpensive

오리

awree

고양이

kaw-yang-ee

쥐

chwee

소

saw

토끼

taw-kkee

개

ke

말

mal

원숭이

won-soong-ee

사자

saja

물고기

moolgaw-gee

코끼리

kaw-kkeeree

양

yang

cat	duck
cow	mouse
dog	rabbit
monkey	horse
fish	lion
sheep	elephant

팔	손가락
pal	*sawn-garak*
머리	입
moree	*eep*
귀	다리
kwee	*taree*
손	배
sawn	*pe*
눈	머리카락
noon	*moree-karak*
코	등
kaw	*tung*

finger	arm
mouth	head
leg	ear
stomach	hand
hair	eye
back	nose